Investing

A Full Beginners' Guide To Starting, Growing, And Succeeding In Business Using Proven Techniques

(An Introduction To Investing And Options Trading For Beginners)

Trevor Manning

TABLE OF CONTENT

Why Make An Investment? 1

Strategies For Day Trading Options 8

How Do Financial Levers Work? 19

Mentality And The Brain 32

Have An Edge 55

How Can I Interact With The Market? 62

How To Approach Business As An Owner 68

Bonds Evaluation 76

The Investor 87

The Business Management Must Be Competent. 102

Understanding The Different Types Of Cryptocurrency 106

How To Invest In Etfs 120

The Value Of Investments 126

Why Make An Investment?

Should I invest or not? The query is that.

What comes to mind when you think of investing?

The concept of investing is extremely similar to gambling for the majority of people. They take a chance on a stock, win big, and all of their issues are resolved. But this is something that only occurs in movies and not in real life. Investing is a deliberate activity in real life. When investments are well planned, returns are often significantly higher than anticipated.

As a result, investment is something we should see as a chance. You will never succeed if you approach investing as a pain now, joy tomorrow proposition. You will be well on your way to building a sizable financial fortune when you decide to invest because you are confident in your ability to meet your goals.

So let's look at the justification for investing.

Increase Your Income

Most people who invest do seek to increase their existing income. It's challenging to support yourself with only one source of income. Furthermore, working longer hours doesn't always result in higher pay. As a result, the majority of individuals search for other ways to augment their monthly income.

Investing becomes important in this situation.

You ultimately get returns on your investments when you invest money. Interest is often paid on a monthly or quarterly basis by common investment vehicles like mutual and index funds. They provide extra money that may be used for a variety of things. The profits you may expect from these investments, however, are often meager.

The returns you get from mutual funds might sometimes be underwhelming. This is the rationale behind why many individuals choose to invest directly in equities. Investors stand to benefit far more by eliminating intermediaries. Day, swing, and position trading are thus used as a means of producing consistent revenue by smart, proactive investors. You have a winning formula that may assist you in funding a pleasant living when you decide to combine your normal income with revenue from investment.

Making retirement plans

This strategy is long-term. Retirement expenditures may be paid for via investment accounts like IRAs and 401(k)s. For those who have the time to spare, these investments are quite effective. Therefore, the more money you stand to earn the younger you start. As a result, you have less time to save for retirement the longer you wait to create one of these accounts.

For individuals trying to save money for retirement, investing in equities makes sense. You may simply roll over investments to increase your nest egg, depending on your plan. You'll eventually accumulate not just a consistent source of income but also a sizeable sum of capital. Stock investment thus makes perfect sense for people who are putting money aside for retirement.

Get Paid While You Sleep

One of the most compelling justifications for investing is passive income. You essentially don't have to labor for your money if you have passive income. Although it may seem too good to be true, this is a reality. You may program your trading system to do the job for you when you invest in stocks. Nowadays, computers are used for almost all trade. You may automate all of your trades with the use of algorithmic trading. As a result, all you have to do is set up your transactions; the system will take care of the rest.

You may dedicate a few hours every day, or perhaps a few days, to your transactions by using automatic trading. After setting everything up, you may relax and observe the proceedings. You must, of course, keep up with the action. However, you won't need to sit in front of the computer for long to do this.

Additionally, some people decide to make trading their full-time profession. You can work both actively and passively, if you so desire. While you divert your attention to others, you may set up transactions to operate automatically. You might say that you are managing many deals simultaneously.

This is the response to the question, "How do stockbrokers make so much money in such a short time?" They do many trades simultaneously by using the capabilities of automated trading.

Become financially independent

You don't need to work to support your lifestyle if you are financially independent. To put it another way, you decide to labor. Not out of need, but out of want, you labor. This is what freedom really means. Additionally, working a job will not help you do this.

People who acquire financial independence do so by making investments in stocks, properties, or businesses. They eventually reach a position where they can live comfortably without working. As a result, they are not dependent on a 9 to 5 job to support themselves. They are supported by an automated system.

You can afford to make time for the things you have always desired once you have financial freedom. Without giving up your time, you may support your loved ones. You may give your health a higher priority than your job. In the end, most individuals desire financial independence as their ultimate objective.

The majority of individuals do, in fact, claim to seek wealth. They are expressing the desire to not have to worry about paying the bills on a monthly basis. The majority of individuals want to a comfortable existence where they have the means to do whatever they please, whenever they please. As a result, they are not fixated on a certain sum of money in their bank account.

You may surely become extremely rich via stock investing if you are interested in doing so. It requires persistence and effort, but the results are worth it. The ideas in this book will assist you in getting there. But you must begin investing right now. Your journey to the promised land will take longer the longer you wait.

Strategies For Day Trading Options

A good strategy would be required if you establish up with a dealer and have your very own trading area ready to go. Day trading strategies exist in a variety of forms, some basic and others more complicated. There are a few crucial elements that will be included in most approaches before we look at an example. Charts and trends may often be used to predict possible pricing changes while doing business online. They are predicated on the core idea that history is repeating itself, and you can find many of successful traders who fervently concur with that idea.

The most recent selling options indications will be claimed by your map. The Put-Call Ratio Tracker, Capital Flow Index, Open Interest, Relative Strength Index, and Bollinger Bands are a few examples of these that differ from strategy to strategy. You'll discover that trading in trends for options requires perseverance and knowledge. Before you locate a chart with data that accurately depicts the situation, you would need to iron out any wrinkles and test out a few alternative ones.

Options with Covered Calls

A call option is a kind of contract option in which the buyer (the holder) has the right but not the duty to acquire a certain amount of a commodity at a specific price within a set window of time (until the option expires).

In the event that the option is exercised, the writer (seller) of a call option is obligated to sell the underlying securities at the strike price. The call choice writer receives a premium for assuming the risk associated with the duty.

100 shares from each transaction come with stock options. If the person who wrote the call option holds the necessary quantity of the security backing it, the short call is protected. The covered call

is a popular option strategy that enables stockholders to generate extra income from their investment in stocks by periodically selling call options. Please review our article on covered call strategy for additional details. As an alternative to writing covered calls with a similar benefit possibility and much less capital need, someone could purchase a bull call spread. The preferred bull call spread method just asks the trader to acquire deep-in-the-money call options; it does not call for the purchase of the underlying shares.

Selling near-month options makes sense when time decay is at its peak since the goal of selling covered calls is to collect premiums. Therefore, the two strategies we compare would involve selling slightly out-of-the-money call options in the next several weeks.

Options for Married Put

With no limit on the underlying stock price increase, both married puts and long calls have the same limitless profit potential. However, because of the price or premium of the acquired option, the benefit is often less than merely holding the stock. When the underlying stock rises by the amount of premium options acquired, the approach reaches break-even. Anything more is considered income.

A married put provides the benefit of lowering the stock's downside risk since it now has a floor. The difference between the underlying stock price at the time the put was purchased and the put strike price is known as the floor. Simply said, if the underlying stock exactly sold at the strike price when the option was purchased, the strategy loss is limited to the exact amount paid for the chance.

Due to its profile, a married put is also known as a long synthetic call. The technique is similar to buying a normal call option (without the underlying stock) since both situations include the same dynamic: little risk and limitless potential for profit. There is no doubt that how much less money a lengthy call costs makes a difference between both strategies.

Opt for a bull call spread

An option to selling covered calls that offers a similar profit prospect but requires far less cash is to purchase bull call spreads. The preferred bull call spread method simply needs the trader to acquire deep-in-the-money call options since the underlying stock of the covered call strategy has already been purchased.

Selling near-month options at the peak of their time decay makes sense if the goal of writing covered calls is to recoup premiums. Therefore, selling call options that are just a little out of the money in the near-month term would be one of the two strategies we compare. The distribution of the bull call lowers the risk of the call option, but at a cost. The stock market returns are likewise limited, creating a narrow range where buyers may profit. Traders will utilize the bull call spread if they anticipate a modest rise in a commodity's price. They'll probably use this strategy when there's a lot of ambiguity.

The bull call distribution consists of two call option-required phases.

Choose the assets you think will increase in value over the next several days, weeks, or months. Purchase a call option with a strike price higher than the selling price for a certain closing date and pay the premium. Another name is a lengthy call when using this alternative. Sell a call option with the same expiration date and higher strike price at the same time as the first call option. A rapid call for this alternative is also known as.

Spread Options for Bear Puts

A bear put spread is a kind of options strategy used when a trader or investor anticipates a modest decline in the price of a security or asset. When selling the same quantity of puts on the same asset at the same expiration date at a lower strike price, bear put propagation is achieved by buying put options. The possible profit with this strategy is the difference between the two strike prices, less the options' net value.

An option for a note is the right to sell a certain amount of the underlying securities at a specified strike price.

often referred to as a long put spread or a debt put spread. A bearish trader who wants to boost revenue while cutting losses would use a bear put spread as an options strategy.

Buying and selling puts on the same underlying asset at the same expiration date but with different strike rates is a bear put spread strategy.

With a decline in the price of the underlying asset, a bear puts spread makes a profit. As a result, the net capital expenditure is less than purchasing a single put outright. Additionally, since the risk is restricted to bear put spread net expenditure, it is far less risky than shorting stocks or purchasing insurance. Selling a stock short theoretically has an unlimited possibility if the price increases. A bear put spread could be the best course of action unless the investor anticipates that the underlying stock or asset will decrease somewhat between the day of settlement and the expiration date. However, the dealer forfeits the ability to request the additional Benefit if the underlying stock or asset decreases by more than. Many traders are attracted by the trade-off between risk and potential reward.

Options for Protective Collars

To lessen downside risk, you may use the protective collar strategy, where you buy some protection options, sell a short call option, and buy a long-placed option. This strategy protects equities from falling market prices. When sold, it employs cash-on-call options, and when bought, a put option.

Everyone else is short securities, and the lender is responsible for covering their positions. When you buy a long put option, you're betting that the stock price will be lower than the expiration strike price. The shares are held by the investor.

Selling the current call option until the investor believes the market price will fall below the call strike point is known as a fast call option. The owner will gain. The buyer must acquire these shares again later when the price drops and compensate the owner even though they won't be their own.

Options for long and short strangles

As the options dealer takes into account the underlying stock and expiration date, the infinite options strangle is a very advantageous, low-risk strategy.

The long strangle option strategy generates significant gains when the underlying stock price makes a substantial move to the upside or downside at expiration. The following is the formula for calculating profit:

When Underlying Price > Long Call Strike Price + Net Premium Paid OR Underlying Price Long Put Strike Price — Net Premium Paid, Maximum Benefit = Unlimited Benefit Gained Earnings are calculated as follows: Long Put Strike Price — Underlying Price — Net Premium Paid OR Long Call Strike Price — Underlying Price — Net Premium Paid

One rapid call with a higher trigger price and one low shot are strangled by a medium. The same underlying supply and expiration date apply to each option, but the strike rates vary. A short strangle is created for a net credit (or net receipt) if the underlying stock moves in a constrained range below the break-even marks. The only available benefits are from accumulating donations that yield lower commissions. If stock demand rises and asset sales fall considerably, the potential liability is unlimited. The only full benefit efficiency is reduced total commission earnings. If the short strangle expires, the stock price trades at or below the strike prices, and all options expire worthless, the investor will get the whole benefit. Given that stock prices may increase indefinitely, the potential for profit loss is endless. When the stock price potentially go to zero, there is a considerable potential danger on the downside.

How Do Financial Levers Work?

The word "leverage" is often used in financial management. It results from using borrowed funds to both extend and finance an investment. After then, it will provide some returns on the risk capital. It is a tactic to make investments utilizing borrowed funds. It boosts the return on the investment. Leverage may also refer to the amount of debt that a business uses to fund its assets. A high level of leverage indicates that the investor has accrued more debt than equity. Leverage is known to improve returns, leading to a rise in profit.

It increases the possible rewards on a certain investment. If the investment you made does not work out as you had hoped, it will reduce the probability to arise. Investors and companies both employ the concept of leverage. An investor will utilize to guarantee that the returns on the investment improve. Utilizing specialized instruments, such as margin accounts, options, and futures, the investment will be leveraged. Leverage will be used by businesses to fund their assets. They choose to employ debt financing to obtain cash rather than issuing shares in an effort to boost shareholder value.

Investors prefer not to employ leverage right away. They have the tools necessary to get at it informally. They choose to invest in a business that they are aware employs force to grow and support its operations. The business is not need to necessarily raise the expenditure. Leverage is a fantastic strategy that everyone may utilize to increase their purchasing power in the market. How

Promotion of Your Offers

Both merchants and buyers are looking forward to your visit!

Get ready to explore this information and learn! You must have a system in place that enables timely, labor- and money-efficient communication with your buyer list. There is no doubt about it: the marketing strategy you use to alert customers to deals will be the foundation of your business.

The advantage of selling properties wholesale to a variety of clients is that each one operates with a different profit margin. The next buyer may think highly of a bargain that the first deems to be average or worse. How does this relate to your marketing strategy and the effectiveness of your assets for wholesale?

It doesn't always mean a house is a bad bargain just because one bidder feels it's marginal. Real estate is more like the proverbial "eye of the beholder" than you may imagine. Given the amazing conditions you have attached to the home (or cash price), one buyer may perceive the property you provided to them as a great deal despite all the work they could do themselves. The following purchaser could be too value-conscious to make a sizable profit and decide against buying.

In any situation, you won't know until you put your target property in front of a lot of potential buyers. The greatest way to explain it was by real estate guru Ron LeGrand: "A few will. Some people won't.Next, what?

The investor will have access to the bulk of the information needed to examine the transaction without having to get in touch with you personally, which is a wonderful benefit of having your marketing plan in place. It will enable the buyer to do their own research before you agree to see them at the subject property and will give them a broad idea of what the conditions or price of the property are.

In negotiations with several sellers, both sides believed they had negotiated hard and made every effort to reach an agreement, but a critical review revealed it to be a marginal, or even non-marginal, accord. You shouldn't be scared to say that the deal is too good to pass up but that you would draw up a contract subject to financing or finding a buyer if you are positive that this is the best price the seller will accept.

When you're up and running, you'll be delivering several properties to your clients simultaneously. If so, it is no longer expensive to include a transaction that you later found to be marginal. That marginal transaction could be wholesaleable for a smaller profit, perhaps $500. However, promoting it didn't cost you anything; all you had to do was connect it into your system. If you think about it, many individuals work 40 hours each week to make $500. Over time, smaller payouts add up. Not much to write home about, but also not exactly pennies on the dollar.

If your marketing plan is correctly implemented, you will swiftly and consistently make money. In fact, if you are persistent in spreading the news to your customers, they will soon be pleading with you for more properties to sell. You want to be dealing with problems like these. Additionally, word spreads quickly among reputable investors, and you will find that others want to be added to your list of buyers so they can be notified when deals are available. Once your marketing strategy is in place, you'll notice that your list of potential customers grows significantly.

The Best Approach to Configuring Your Marketing System

Setting up your marketing strategy will need some time and effort in addition to these suggestions. We'll go through the basics of what you should do to put your target properties in front of prospective buyers as soon as feasible.

The deadline is as follows: 15 minutes. You must advise your buyers within 15 minutes of any time you have knowledge of a property that is prepared for wholesale.

You need a computer system in order to advertise efficiently. If you are not using a computer at work, you are not in business. If you don't have one, can you wholesale? Yes, of course. But doing so is equivalent to trying to win a motor race while mounted. He may ultimately complete the circuit, but a motorized vehicle would make the experience much more pleasurable. Don't restrict yourself, then. You must use the most recent technology accessible since you are in business.

Anyone may wholesale a home from beginning to end with a few qualified buyers since all the essential information is in our books. You could even find that your buyer marketing approach consists just of a five-person list in your black book.

But here is where things start to get interesting for those of you who are serious about wholesaling a lot of properties and want to attain the highest success rate on the transactions you finish. You want to convey to your customers that you have a deal that is so good that if they wait to contact you for further information, it could already be too late for them to take advantage of it.

Comparing it to fishing is the simplest way to explain the kind of marketing plan you will use. You see, there is a certain percent probability that you will catch a fish if you throw only one line into the water. That's OK if you're trying to relax.

Have you ever seen the lengthy lines used by commercial fishermen? They always have a large number of hooks available. They have a considerably better chance of catching fish than the guy with only one line out, you can be sure of that.

The same reasoning holds true for your marketing plan, as your success rate in wholesaling properties will be directly correlated to how quickly you can spread your message and how many various media outlets you use to inform your customers. The amount of customers you send the letter to will be the final consideration.

If you want to implement an effective marketing plan, you will need or have access to the following:

A device that can process written documents

Nothing extra is required for this. Anything that enables you to summarize your subject property in one paragraph.

a printing apparatus

You can send out a ton of letters and postcards online without ever touching any paper! This is a need, however, if you don't have access to the internet.

High-speed access to the internet

This is a need if you don't want to deal with letters or postcards.

An AFX number

Although you are not allowed to send out fax alerts of your subject properties, you should do so because despite the popularity of email, sometimes the more traditional ways still get people's attention. You don't want to miss out on this chance to get in touch with a buyer. If you do, resist the urge to sit at the machine and serve your many different customers the same item again. There is a way that is far more effective.

Keep in mind that the whole process of reaching your customers just takes 15 minutes.

Mentality And The Brain

I'm sorry if you've already read Afterlife: Powerful Evidence You Won't Lose. This chapter will provide an overview of a lecture I also authored. Bruce Greyson is a doctor. was the University of Virginia's Division of Perceptual Studies Director and Chester Carlson Professor of Psychiatry at the time. He was paid to research awareness. Dr.

Greyson is now an Emeritus Professor.

Contrary to what scientists think, Dr. Greyson's speech demonstrates that awareness is not produced by brains. He does, however, concede that it is conceivable to think that the brain may produce awareness. Consider what happens when someone consumes too much alcohol or has a head injury. The electrical activity of the brain during different mental processes may be measured. This makes it possible to discover connections between various brain regions and activities. Different parts of the brain may be stimulated, recorded, and then observed to see how they impact behavior. Although this raises the possibility that the brain plays a role in cognition, perception, and memory, Dr. Greyson points out that this does not necessarily imply that the brain is the source of these ideas. In contrast to causality, the measurements reveal correlations. In reality, thoughts, perceptions, and memories take place elsewhere. Then, the brain interprets them in a manner like to that of a radio receiver, television, or mobile phone.

Western science, according to Dr. Greyson, is primarily reductionist. It breaks everything down into its constituent parts, which makes studying the entire simpler. The components don't always function like the whole, however. A single neuron cannot generate a thought, feel furious, or feel cold, despite the fact that the brain is made up of millions of nerve cells, or neurons. Brain cells are capable of feeling and thinking, but they cannot act. How many neurons are needed to produce an idea is unknown. We also don't know how many neurons can cooperate.

By arguing that consciousness is an emergent trait in brains, scientists have discovered a means to get past this issue. When sufficient numbers of brain cells are combined, this characteristic appears. According to Dr. Greyson, calling anything an emergent quality denotes that it cannot be explained. It is well established that there is no process in the brain that creates non-physical entities like ideas, memories, and sensations. The issue of how electrical impulses or chemical triggers in the brain may form ideas, emotions, or, for that matter, any other thing the mind produces, is left unanswered by materialistic worldviews. According to Dr. Greyson, scientists continue to think that the brain creates consciousness in a mysterious way that is beyond our comprehension.

Dr. Greyson said that although most people believed that the mind and brain were distinct up until roughly a century ago, scientists in the West started to investigate the idea that thinking and consciousness may originate from the physical brain. Ironically, scientists from the field of physics had to give up Newtonian physics and invent quantum mechanics in order to explain situations where consciousness--what a researcher doesn't know--was involved.

--totally modifies the outcomes of several investigations. It seems as if the right hand was operating independently of the left. It's incredible that things still work this way now.

In his talk, Dr. Greyson emphasized the data that the Division of Perceptual Studies' investigators, who started working there in 1967, had gathered to demonstrate that consciousness may exist independently of the brain. This demonstrates the obstinacy and incapacity of materialist scientists. Over the course of fifty years, Dr. Greyson and his associates have been gathering this data, and several articles have been published that expose a great deal of it. The majority of scientists in the West are unaware of this information, nevertheless. You will soon be able to surpass many scientists in the West.

Four different categories of evidence exist:

1. Long-term unconsciousness may cause people to regain consciousness only hours or days before they pass away.

2. Some persons with little brain tissue may nonetheless be capable of complicated awareness.

3. Complex awareness when the brain isn't working well or at a very low level, and during near-death experiences.

4. Memories are accurate in recalling information from a previous life, especially in youngsters. Deathbed regaining of lost consciousness

Since more than 250 years ago, people with neurological and behavioral illnesses have reportedly experienced an unexpected improvement in their mental clarity. Medical literature has described patients who had meningitis, strokes, or brain tumors or abscesses. These patients had long since lost the capacity to speak or reason. Brain scans and autopsy performed on several of these individuals revealed severe and irreparable brain damage. However, in many instances, in the last moments, hours, and perhaps days before their passing, mental clarity was restored. 83 examples have been found by the Division of Perceptual Studies in western medical literature. It also contains unpublished testimonies of patients who passed away but then fully recovered their awareness. Clarity has returned, and the patient's brain appears to have loosened its hold.

German doctor Julius wrote in 1844 that this illness claimed the lives of 13% of his patients. An year old man was diagnosed with a malignant brain tumor that rapidly worsened, according to a recent study of the end-of-life experiences in Britain. Seventy percent of nursing home caregivers reported witnessing patients with dementia and confusion completely lose their condition. He had one eye blindness, became illogical, weird, and bedridden. He would smack his family like an insect since he was unable to understand his environment. All night long, he would talk incoherently and finally quit sleeping. After many weeks, he suddenly relaxed and began to talk clearly. He comfortably slept off. The next morning when he awoke, he remained still. After he ceased talking, he passed away.

There is no known physiological mechanism that may account for this behavior. Although rare, this phenomena cannot account for how the brain functions. This shows that there may be more nuance in the relationship between consciousness and brain function than most scientists realize. It's as if the brain is wounded, preventing communication, but as the brain starts to die, awareness returns.

Complex awareness may exist in people with very little brain tissue.

Thirdly, persons with relatively little brain tissue may have normal intellect or even high intelligence. People who seem to be able to operate properly and have normal IQ do occur in rare but exceptional circumstances. 2007 saw the publication of one case. It concerned a Smith College-accepted high school honors student. She was rendered unconscious after suffering injuries in a vehicle accident. She didn't have a cerebral cortex, according to a skull x-ray. There was just a brainstem in her skull. When the patient's skull was opened for surgery, the physician discovered a brainstem within.

Neurologists believe that the brainstem carries sensory and motor information from the cerebellum to the spinal cord. Additionally, it incorporates respiration, consciousness, and cardiac function. Higher cognitive activities like thinking, seeing, and making choices cannot be performed by the brainstem. The college-bound honor student shouldn't have been able to generate any thoughts at this point, much less operate at a high intellectual level.

This incident is not unique. Numerous incidences of hydrocephalus in which 95 percent of the brain was impacted by cerebrospinal fluid were described by Dr. Greyson. Nevertheless, many people with this degree of disability have normal or even higher IQs.

Almost Fatal Experiences

In his talk, Dr. Greyson discussed near-death experiences (NDEs) that people who had been pronounced clinically dead and subsequently been brought back to life or resuscitated have shared. They often have intense sensory recollections and visuals. In the words of many, the experience was "more real" than normal living. This occurs in the context of significantly changed brain function, which the materialist model would see as being impossibly unlikely. Between 10 and 20% of patients who have been brought back to life after passing away claim to have these recollections. More than a thousand instances have been looked at by Dr. Greyson directly.

The average age of these patients at the time was 31 years. There were several others, however. A small child spoke about her eight-month-old experience during kidney surgery. The majority of the experiences Dr. Greyson has seen were near death. He had a heart attack and passed away at the age of 81. Surgery accounted for one-third of all NDEs, severe sickness for 25%, and life-threatening accidents for 25%. Changes in thought and emotion are characteristics of NDEs. They may also have supernatural or otherworldly characteristics.

The perception that time is changing might be a sign of a shift in thinking. Many individuals assert that time has stopped or that reality has vanished. Another aspect of the shift in thinking phenomena was a sudden insight or knowledge that made everything in the cosmos appear very obvious. The individual had the impression that their thinking was more rapid and coherent than usual. Finally, a full life review became available to the individual, and a timeline of their lifetimes flashed before their eyes.

The overwhelming sensation of calm and well-being, the perception that everything is in harmony, the feeling of oneness with everything, total pleasure, and unconditional love were some of the most prevalent feelings.

An out-of-body experience is one of the characteristics of the paranormal. This is referred to as an OBE (out of body experience). Your bodily senses, such as sight and hearing, seem to be more vivid than ever. Sometimes, people claim to hear noises and colors that aren't there in our reality. Additionally, they assert having extrasensory perception. This entails that individuals are able to see and hear things that are ordinarily out of reach for their senses, such as faraway happenings. Finally, some persons claim to have seen future visions and to have been taken to another dimension or domain of existence.

Many claim to have reached a point when they were unable to continue. They would be unable to return home if they passed this line, which was designated as a point of no return. A lot of individuals also claim to have seen a supernatural or spiritual person. Some people even claim that they have witnessed deceased loved ones being welcomed into another planet or that they have been brought back to life.

Psychiatrist Dr. Greyson is especially interested in the lasting impact of NDEs. Near-death experiencers often describe predictable patterns of changes in their views, convictions, and values that do not seem to become smaller with time. They assert that as a result of their encounters, they are now more spiritual. Additionally, they claim to feel more sympathy and a stronger want to aid others. Most responders state that they don't dread death and that they think we can endure it. The majority of respondents—nearly half—state that material goods are no longer important to them. Many claim that they are no longer interested in pursuing fame, prestige, or excellence.

According to Dr. Greyson, NDEs cannot bring about awareness. Three characteristics of NDEs, according to him, point to this: 1) increased mental function when the brain is disabled; 2) accurate perceptions outside the body, such as the capacity to communicate with medical personnel about what they see and hear in the operating room; and 3) encounters in which the deceased provide precise information that no one else can know. NDE survivors sometimes get the chance to interact with the deceased.

Despite having meningitis, a nine-year-old kid had an NDE. His sister, who was among the numerous departed relatives he encountered, counseled him to go back to his body. As soon as he got back from his death, he notified his parents, who had been at his side the whole time for 36 hours. His father was really disturbed that his apparently healthy daughter was attending college in another state. He said that his sister had urged him to go home and insisted that she remain.

He made a commitment to his wife before leaving the hospital that he would contact their daughter when he got home. His daughter was nowhere to be found despite his best efforts. The college administrators had been attempting to get in touch with him all night so they could break the heartbreaking news to him. At midnight, their daughter was murdered in a car accident.

By searching for "Dr Bruce Greyson consciousness unaffected by the brain" on YouTube, you may also discover a video of Dr. Greyson's presentation there.

Kids Who Remember a Past Life

Dr. Greyson also discussed the Division of Perceptual Studies' investigation into children's past-life memories. Over fifty years have passed since these studies began at the University of Virginia. In their files, there are more than 2500 examples. I was completely aware of this before to Dr. Greyson's speech. The reason I was acquainted with it was because I had done study on it for REINCARNATION, Good News for Open Minded Christians (and other Truth Seekers). One of the main researchers in the Perceptual Division is the child psychiatrist Jim B. Tucker (M.D.). He has published two books regarding the reincarnation study being done by the Division. He agreed to two interviews with me.

It will be challenging to deny that reincarnation is possible if you are open-minded and consider the evidence. Numerous accounts are anecdotal. You may remember Glenn Ford, a famous actor from Hollywood's Golden Age (1916–1906). Ford chose to study more about the paranormal after being asked by a producer to play a role in a movie about Peter Hurkos (1911–1988). Ford, who was 54 at the time, saw Hurkos perform and spoke with specialists. Ford willingly had three hypnosis-based former life regression sessions in December 1975. He also spoke about his prior five lifetimes. While under hypnosis, Glenn Ford was carried back to his early years and encouraged to remember his former life.

Ford once identified himself as Charles Stewart of Elgin, Scotland, a single music instructor who had passed away in 1892. Although Stewart loved horses, he detested his work as a piano instructor for schoolgirls. Amazingly, Ford was able to play music under hypnosis, including sections from Beethoven and Mozart. Ford claimed to be an expert with horses and to share Stewart's passion for them. He said that given his present situation, he was unable to play the piano and would not do so. After the past-life regression sessions, researchers traveled to Scotland to look for historical data regarding Charles Stewart of Elgin (a Scottish music instructor who passed away in 1892).

Ford's second hypnotic regression session brought back recollections of his time serving in the elite horse cavalry of French King Louis XIV. Under hypnosis, Ford was able to speak French with ease.

Additionally, he provided detailed details regarding France in the year 300.

Ford was then taken back in time to previous life. He spoke of a Christian martyr who was devoured by lions in the Coliseum of third-century Rome and a Royal Navy sailor who perished in the Great Plague in the 17th century. Ford raised cattle in the American West as a cowboy. Ford appeared as a star in 106 films and several TV shows, including comedies, police dramas, and war tales. However, he was most known for playing a cowboy in Western movies.

What does this say about you personally? In the more than 200 years since the first Homo sapiens roamed the earth, you have experienced many different lives. If this is the case, it is likely that you have been evolving, although slowly in some cases and more swiftly in others. You've taken on different guises, such as that of a fighter or a victor. Your subconscious mind, which Christians refer to as your soul, contains all of the knowledge and experience you have acquired. This book tries to guide you to the inner champion.

Another thing to keep in mind is that you may have had brown, white, or black skin at various points in your life. This should demonstrate how silly racism is. You've been a lady at times and a guy at others. It's possible that you have experience with the opposite sex, which might help to explain why you don't feel comfortable having sex right now. You can have unexplainable phobias, predilections, or anxieties. This could be the result of experiences or prior programming. According to UVa studies, this happens often. Whatever the case may be, everything you have ever known is now a part of you, or what some would refer to as your subconscious mind and others, as your Higher Self or Soul.

The goal of this life—and all the lifetimes you have left—is to improve who you are. The aim is self-actualization. It's for self-actualization. This is the secret to contentment and leading a life that is really meaningful. In this lifetime, your ego self and Higher Self should work together to foster a cooperative attitude. More information will be covered in this chapter. We shall state at the end of this chapter that we have always been completely integrated components of the Infinite Mind, or the collective awareness. We each have an endless awareness, and we are nearly infinitely capable. It is up to each of us to decide how much self-actualization or progress we can do to fulfill this potential.

Let me give you a different explanation. You are an immortal unit of mind that may continue to develop indefinitely after being formed. You may do this by choosing your own route, developing it, and then pursuing it. You may remember from the Foreword that Jesus is recorded as stating in John 10:34 (NIV), "Is it not written into your Law, "I have stated that you are "gods""," in reference to Psalm 8:6.

A zeitgeist is a group of people who realize who they are and what they can do, and this will bring about incredible prosperity for themselves and the country. Imagine that you are a god, it's an amazing realization and thought, but it's true, and this means that you can achieve whatever you believe and imagine you can.

Have An Edge

Being an investor implies being competitive by nature. In spite of the fact that investment produces real wealth, some of your short-term gains will be offset by the losses of others. Simply relying on market measures and indicators is insufficient. Every investor has access to these resources. You need to take some action that sets you apart from the crowd and offers you an advantage over rivals.

The edge just has to be sharp enough to cut beyond the first layer of less knowledgeable investors; it doesn't need to be a magic trick or a well-developed algorithm that you created yourself. Simply put, you do not want to fall into the category of investors who lose the most money. This is significant because it presents the difficulty in a more clearer manner. Instead of competing with Warren Buffet, choose a person who is on an equal footing with you. Even while every investor has access to stock market indicators, it's how you utilize those metrics that might provide you an advantage over other investors. For instance, using the advance/decline line correctly might provide you with more information that helps you make money. The advance-decline line is often used by investors to assess the performance of the market as a whole, but fewer individuals build their own stock indexes and compare these more specialized advance/decline ratios. It seems like a lot of complicated math to discover a trending segment of the market by working with a portion of the market, but it's not. You are only measuring something that everyone else is ignoring using a technology that is accessible to everyone. There is undoubtedly a skill involved in knowing which stocks should be examined simultaneously, but you can start using this gift right now without needing to spend years in school or learn complex arithmetic.

Other instances of designing the ideal investment environment need not be as reliant on data. Some traders may discover they just have a competitive advantage when shorting equities. Some people will be naturally inclined to acquire inexpensive stocks and then sell them. These great traders have identified their inherent skills and are investing their time in developing them. These are not extraordinary talents and do not need years of education or hours of research. It is impossible to quantify why another investor is more successful when he buys inexpensive companies. The quantity of time available for investment may be one of the criteria that determine this skill; maybe their constrained time is truly the secret to their success. This investor is really giving oneself a huge advantage by being on a schedule that only permits checking the market figures twice each day. The key to success is in discovering this skill via exploration. You must evaluate your behaviors in order to get an objective assessment of your skills. Just remember that most individuals will think they are above average; if you can gauge your skills just a little bit more properly, you will have an advantage.

Dow's Canines

The Dogs of the DOW trading strategy may be the most simple and successful trading strategy ever. This concept, made famous by Michael Higgins in the book "Beating the Dow," demonstrates how a simple approach may produce amazing outcomes. Higgins was able to examine the market and develop his own program utilizing the existing measurements. He would examine at the top 30 Dow Jones Industrial companies with the biggest dividends before investing equally in the top 10 of those firms. His strategy was to always own equal shares of the stocks with the greatest dividends. For the investor who cannot commit hours each day to market monitoring, the maintenance of this strategy is lovely. Only three to four times a year would investments need to be moved.

The efficiency of Higgins' approach is evident. The top ten equities paying the greatest dividends beat the Dow as a whole by around 3% when applied to the Dow between 1957 and 2003. The Dow returned an average of 11%

throughout this time, whereas the dogs returned an astounding 14.3% yearly. Although it seems to reason that the companies paying the largest dividends will provide the biggest returns, the investment is made after the stock's data has been made public. In essence, you are continually getting in after the stock has already reached its previous high point. Since it may be improved, Dog of the Dow has undergone several variations. There are methods for investing in a small number of stocks that employ the top five stocks, the top four stocks, or various ratios. The approach works because it makes intuitive sense, and that's the key point. It always makes intuitive sense that there are gains being lost since the current approach isn't flawless, which is why the methodology gets improved.

You don't need to use an approach as daring as Michael Higgins' to choose profitable stocks in the market. The fact that you are patient and exclusively invest in government bonds and index funds may be to your advantage. Although it may not seem like an advantage in terms of investing, these kinds of secure investments really perform far better in the long run than buying individual equities. It's crucial to note that you are using a strategy that you are familiar with, one that works for your needs, your financial situation, and the amount of time you have available to invest in the markets.

How Can I Interact With The Market?

How then can you determine which kind of platform is the best match for your business? Companies having a sizable pool of intellectual property and a targeted audience within a certain industry may find it advantageous to partner with an augmented platform. These specialized platforms may draw on their specialized experience to guarantee a successful launch and produce additional value via secondary tools and services. A higher amount of monetizable content often indicates a larger upfront investment that is more likely to pay off.

It's worth looking at other creators' NFT projects for inspiration if you're unsure of what kinds of specialized services will be a good fit for your company. For instance, artists may use these platforms to provide unique video content, or sports teams may offer free meet-and-greets or VIP upgrades with NFT purchases. Recently, McLaren Racing introduced a promotion where fans could gather various digital parts of a Formula 1 race car. The first fan to collect all 22 of the NFTs needed to create a full digital version of the car would win a trip to a Formula 1 race, expenses included.

Additionally, some enhanced systems include in-depth data analytics on when other NFTs on the market were minted, how many NFT competitors are minted, average prices, sales numbers, and more. Companies may utilize this information to make educated decisions about how to manage and price their own digital offerings. For instance, NBA Top Shot provides a detailed statistics page for each NFT that contains information on the video highlight's ownership history, related market activity, and other factors. Similar to this, the electronic music market place RCRDSHP provides customers with extensive analytics on both individual NFTs and the state of the market as a whole. These industry-specific platforms may have a narrower reach, but they may be quite successful in a certain market; for instance, Sorae generated over $100 million in the previous year and close to $20 million in transaction volume last month.

But for products with a wider audience, businesses and artists could be better off cooperating with a specialized market. For instance, Coca-Cola collaborated with OpenSea to auction off a "Loot Box" NFT that included digital versions of an antique Coca-Cola cooler, a bag, and a logo, as well as a real, fully-stocked Coca-Cola refrigerator sent to the winner's house. It was a straightforward offering that didn't need much in the way of customer-specific industry specialization, so OpenSea's cloud-based platform was a good fit. (The NFT collection eventually sold for about $575,000. Cocca-Cla donated the money to Special Olympics International.)

What is ahead for us?

You could be asking yourself at this point which of these several platforms is most likely to become the industry standard, a la Amazon. Traditional markets often exhibit winner-takes-all dynamics, which means that once one platform reaches a certain scale, it becomes very impossible for rivals to overcome it. As a result, it is only natural to be concerned about investing in a platform that won't become obsolete. But unlike conventional markets, we think that no one NFT platform is likely to take on such a dominant position. There are two primary reasons for this:

First off, NFT markets are by nature more open than those of their traditional counterparts. Because NFTs are developed on fully public networks, Infrastructure limits the extent to which these platforms may create the kind of data moats that lead to monopolies by making the majority of transaction data publicly accessible.

Additionally, the success of augmented platforms indicates that differentiation is very valuable to both buyers and sellers. We have already seen that there is a significant need for a number of already operating NFT marketplaces, each of which focuses on a different domain and provides specialized tools to assist its participants in succeeding. Multiple platforms may coexist within sectors as long as they vary in the tools and experiences they provide. For instance, one NFT art platform may specialize on minting functionality while another may concentrate on gaming experiences built on top of art NFTs.

While winner-take-all dynamics may be more likely among standardized platforms, where the market place that offers the lowest cost of transactions will likely attract the majority of buyers and sellers, these platforms will never provide the level of customization and industry-specific support made possible by a wide array of regulated platforms. And investors seem to concur: While streamlined platforms have undoubtedly performed well, augmented platforms have also had little trouble attracting funding, with Dapper Labs achieving a valuation of $7.6 billion and Sorae raking in a record-breaking $680 million at a valuation of $4.3 billion.

Don't feel like you have to wait for the "Amazon of NFTs" to appear if you're a creator. Evaluate the current markets based on how well they fit with your particular offerings and business needs, and if you find one that appears well-suited for you, go ahead and dive in.

While NFTs are still a burglary-related industry, they have shown that they have the potential to be very profitable, creating real value for both buyers and sellers. NFTs may have begun as a science project driven mostly by crypto enthusiasts and risk-taking, tech-savvy artists, but they are now quickly entering the mainstream. Whether you're a well-known company like the NBA or a budding independent artist, working with the right platform is the crucial first step to fostering customer engagement and securing your position in this new digital economy.

How To Approach Business As An Owner

You've made the decision to try your hand at real estate investment, but in addition to the knowledge you'll need to make sure you're investing in the correct property and don't take on more than you can handle, you'll also need to learn how to think like an investor.

Real estate investment offers many chances for success and potential rewards. It will, however, take some time for you to completely understand how you should think in order to make sure that your investments are profitable.

Make sure you understand the transaction and your part in it first.

When it comes to the transaction you are working on or your role in that deal, you shouldn't cut any corners. You will be peppered with inquiries about the property you are trying to buy. When trying to sell or rent the property to someone else, you must also make sure you are up to date on all the information about it.

When you first consider the property as an investment, be sure to ask for the most current plans, pictures, drawings, and everything else you need to know in order to fully understand the property and get to know it.

These inquiries shouldn't come as a surprise to the borrower, just as they shouldn't come as a surprise to you when showing the property to a prospective renter. If they are, it is likely that they are hiding something or do not completely understand the property.

The moment has come to hunt for a new employment if they are unable to respond to the queries.

Recognize that needs will be there for both sides.

Try to wait until you get the greatest deal. You shouldn't be forced to give in only to have a quick transaction. If you approach the negotiation with a mindset of compromise, you risk losing the conversation and agreeing to something you do not want.

Here, you need to think like a borrower to understand that the loan requirements are satisfied; otherwise, the agreement won't be useful.

They are also trying to close the transaction with you, therefore the borrower's loan requirements must be satisfied. Therefore, think about both of your needs and goals rather than just your own so that you can create the essential conditions to guarantee that the sale is concluded and you both receive what you need and want.

Obtain the necessary protection

Dealing with a real estate transaction has the advantage that the loan will be backed by the actual property. Once you are aware of this, you may barter without being concerned that you'll need to recalculate your loan-to-value ratio. As a result, the transaction will be closer to your comfort level, and you will be able to make sure that it is completed appropriately for you.

Verify that you consider the danger.

Before investing a lot of money and committing to a property for a long time, you should have a look at it to determine its true value and if it will still be worthwhile in a few years after you have tenants in the home.

Additionally, what if you decide to put the house up for sale?

Will the property's worth increase or decrease? Will it really sell?

How challenging would it be for you to rent out the property?

You should take into account all of these issues before signing a contract with a property. No matter how wonderful the property may seem, bear in mind that there will be things that happen that you cannot control.

Recognize the market

This can result in a failed sale. If you purchase while the market is weak, even after you've put more effort into fixing it up, you won't be able to sell the home. Make sure you are able to read the market to ascertain when it is best for you to purchase and sell.

Be sensible when it comes time to sell.

Back to market expertise again. You risk having a period in which you lose money rather than make it if you don't know when the best moment to sell is.

Make sure that the area is one that others will want to live in as well. You will be left with a home that you spent money on and won't be able to recover your investment if the neighborhood is one that people will want to live in. If people don't want to live in the area, no one will want to purchase it.

Your emotions are important, but you must control them.

Some people won't concur with what you're expressing. Just keep in mind that you are helping someone locate housing, therefore it is crucial that you look out for both of your needs. Do not allow your emotions influence what you are trying to do.

You'll have a smoother transaction and won't have to worry about losing money if you can control your emotions. When you can assist someone in finding housing without having to worry about incurring financial loss, it's a huge gain.

Bonds Evaluation

Important functions in the bond investing aspect to comprehend

Avoid pursuing yield. Going chasing yield is the worst mistake security financial supporters ever made. This will often occur when borrowing costs are low or have just decreased, or when investors feel they are not getting the rate of return they require.

Avoid being seduced by higher returns offered by bonds with worse credit features, or concentrate just on profits from the previous time period. One of the numerous factors a financial supporter should consider when buying securities is yield. Additionally, always keep in mind that increased risk goes along with larger returns.

Describe your objectives. Is your business's goal to raise money for your child's graduate degree? Is it your goal to lead a comfortable retirement? In the event that this is accurate, how quickly? You probably have a lot of goals. Lay them out firmly and precisely as you can. Remember: You won't arrive if you have even the slightest notion where you're heading.

Analyze your level of danger. Similar to stocks and stock assets, different securities and security reserves express different risk profiles. Always be aware of the risks before you participate. It's a good idea to capture them all so they can be seen together.

Finish your task. If you've made it this far, you're looking terrific so far. But keep going. Recognize books and articles about bond investing. Look for information online or go to your local library. Start reading the fixed-pay editorial that appears in newspapers and on financial news programs. Learn more about bond mathematics. You should read the contribution announcement for the bond. You may find all of a security's important characteristics there, from regard to the bond's call strategy.

If you're considering buying a security reserve, carefully read the overview. Pay close attention to the sections that go through the assets' security. An administration security reserve, for instance, contains securities other than government bonds. Pay particular attention to fees. Individual bonds also have descriptions, which are based on the bond's agreement, a legal document that details the terms of the agreement between the bond buyer and bond seller. To understand it, ask your merchant for a copy of the plan or agreement.

Find a company that specializes in bonds if you're buying individual bonds. Talk to numerous agents and choose one that you are satisfied with. Make sure the intermediary is familiar with your travel plans and risk tolerance. Utilize FINRA Broker Check to look up merchant credentials and disciplinary history.

Ask your agent when the bond was last exchanged and for what amount. This can help you comprehend the bond's liquidity (an illiquid bond may not have traded in days or even weeks), as well as the gravity of the firm's appraisal.

View all costs involved in buying and selling bonds. Ask up front how commissions, markups, or markdowns are being used to compensate your financing business and dealer for the transaction.

Invest your coupons again. This enables the power of compounding to erode your advantage. Before you start receiving coupons, it's a good idea to set up a "coupon account" so that you have somewhere to put the money and are not tempted to spend it. You don't need to worry about this, assuming you are acquiring a security reserve, since the asset takes care of this for you.

Avoid trying to time the market. Avoid speculating on borrowing expenses.

Decisions are often made based on where rates have been rather than where they are headed. All things considered, stick to the strategy for speculating that will help you the most in reaching your goals and targets.

INTEREST RATES AND BOND INVESTMENT

There are three fundamental rules that govern what borrowing fees signify for bond costs:

When financing costs increase, bond costs often decrease.

When loan fees decrease, bond costs often increase.

Each security has the risk of lending cost.

One of the key factors affecting bond return is variations in loan costs.

We want to start with the bond's coupon in order to find out why. This is the bond's interest payment. How is that special coupon rate determined? The government finance rate, which handles an account with excessive savings at a Central bank charge various banks that want immediate loans, is one of the major factors. By buying and selling Treasury safeguards, the national bank maintains its target lending cost and establishes an aim for the government to subsidize the rate.

When the national bank acquires safeguards, bank savings increase and government subsidies often cause rates to decline. When the national bank sells safeguards, bank holdings diminish and interest rates will often rise as a result of government subsidies. Although the Fed doesn't directly regulate this rate, it may be effectively controlled via the buying and selling of insurance. Thus, the government financing rate affects lending costs throughout the country, including rates on security coupons.

The Fed Discount Rate, which is the rate at which part banks may get temporary assets from a Central Bank, is another rate that has a significant influence on a security's coupon. It plainly has influence over this rate. Imagine that the Central Bank increases the markdown rate by 0.5 percent. The Central Bank Treasury will logically value its safeguards to reflect the increased borrowing cost the next time it has a closeout for new Treasury securities.

What happens to the Treasury securities you bought at the cheaper borrowing rate two or three months ago? They lack the same allure. If you must sell them, you must keep their price within a range that is greater than the coupon of the proportional number of new securities that were recently issued with the higher rate. Thus, you would have to sell your bonds at a discount.

The alternative method also works. Let's say you bought a $1,000 security with a 6% coupon a few years ago and decided to sell it three years later to pay for a trip to see your ailing grandfather; at that point, loan interest rates were at 4%. Currently, this bond is quite attractive compared to other groups, and you would have the ability to sell it for more money than usual.

Basic Premise Points

Premise focuses, or bps for short, is a phrase that is widely used in reference to securities and finance expenses. One hundredth of a rating point (.01) is a premise point. The predicate 1 percent equals 100 is used. 50% of 1% is 50 premise focuses. securities traders and dealers often utilize premise focuses to make brief comparisons between securities yields. The Central Bank often uses the abbreviation "bps" to refer to fluctuations in the government-subsidy rate.

Bonds carry risk, and that must be understood. the possibility of losing the investment one has made. It is crucial for the investor to be aware of all potential risks before making a bond investment.

The Investor

As was already said, there are many different strategies to generate money on the stock market. You may be wondering, though, how you might develop a reputation as a stock market investor.

You must first decide what role you want to play in the market before you can respond to that question. Your success in the stock market depends on your ability to understand your position. In this chapter, we'll discuss the important objectives you may want to achieve in the market as well as the tools you'll need to establish a name for yourself there.

Which Investing Style Do You Possess?

Stock exchange investing is a reasonably easy skill to master. On the other hand, every individual buys and sells stock for a number of reasons. The amount of risk you want to take on a regular basis, the amount of research you can and want to do on each investment, your level of knowledge or ability to make predictions about the direction of the economy as a whole, and the length of your intended stay in the market all have an impact on the investor you will be.

That seems a little confusing, don't you think? Investors may be grouped into three groups to make things simpler:

Engaged Investors

One of the busiest and most cautious people in the stock market today is an active investor. Before making a purchase, they spend hours analyzing every stock choice, monitoring market trends, and reading the news.

In this instance, their main goals are neither purchasing or selling. They monitor market trends and make judgments based on them. Despite not making long-term investments, they make sure that each one is beneficial.

Passive Traders

The passive investor wants more realistic profits and generally a stress-free stay in the market, as opposed to other investors who aim for the best possible return on each investment. As long as they are having fun trading, these investors don't mind spending more for each investment.

Since others do the tedious effort, passive investors commonly select mutual funds to swiftly diversify their holdings. They stay with what has been shown to be profitable rather than investing their money in new businesses.

Their ultimate goal is to compete in the market with the least amount of effort necessary. If their stock assets have increased in value by at least 20% after they were initially purchased, they may start selling them. Whether a less expensive alternative exists has no bearing. Making things as easy as possible is the main objective for the passive investor.

The Swindler

There is money to be made slowly and there is money to be made on the stock market. Similar to active investors, speculators perform research but focus on equities that are anticipated to have a substantial price gain because of an impending shift. It's possible that a merger between two businesses may raise the price of their shares.

If they knew which stocks were expected to rise, they would buy them before the move occurred. They'll sell the stocks at a greater price if prices increase. Then they repeat the procedure over and again.

Speculators engage in the most trading of all types of investors. This suggests that they sell some assets as soon as a price shift takes place rather than holding them for extended periods of time.

The Deal Seeker

The bargain hunter concentrates on locating inexpensive stocks and keeping them, as opposed to most investors who concentrate on buying low and selling high.

They are mainly focused on long-term growth rather than short-term earnings, particularly when a failing business has a chance of turning things around.

`Despite what we learned in the previous chapter, investors looking for a deal preserved a lot of the firms that were able to stabilize themselves on the stock market. For instance, KMart had such terrible problems that they were essentially removed off Wall Street. However, investments from bargain hunters helped them to escape their predicament.

Someone who approaches the game like a gambler is known as a deal hunter. There is no assurance that a failing business will turn around. But if it does, a shopper may profit much from doing so.

The Investing Veteran

These investors are in the market for the long haul, and as they age, they do adopt different strategies. An investor of this sort may, for instance, start purchasing high-risk equities at an early age and be very active. As individuals age, they become more relaxed and begin to reduce their risks.

As soon as the investor enters retirement age, they will focus on dividend stocks to supplement their monthly income. This investor's survival is a result of their effective risk management. When they are young, they focus on quickly increasing the value of their assets, and as they become older, they change their priorities to make lasting investments.

The Performer

More than any other investing job available, this investor is more like a gambler. They attempt to capitalize on the fact that there will always be volatility and unpredictability in every market.

Regardless of how they do it, the player's objective is to accumulate money as rapidly as they can. The player will be at the forefront whenever a new company enters the market or important changes are made, seeking to benefit from the excitement. If they are confident in the value, they will sell before the market stabilizes.

Although it is a high-risk strategy, the gains often surpass the hazards. If you schedule your investments well, you may be able to benefit from unforeseen opportunities without incurring significant losses.

Who Are You as a Trader?

Trading and investing are two different processes. In fact, there are significant differences between this activity's requirements and dynamics and investment.

You must thus comprehend the kind of traders who are now successful on the market.

a Scalper

Scalpers in the stock market are just traders who are in it to accomplish short-term objectives, despite the fact that the word has some negative connotations these days. They can respond more quickly than day traders and like to concentrate on very specific market areas.

Due to their ability to switch between stocks quickly, scalpers don't need a lot of cash. They will need to have a steady flow of cash on hand, however, in order to profit from market changes.

Their money is little, and as a result, so is their intended profit. They give more weight to incremental improvements that, over time, build up to a large amount. To better understand scalpers, think of them as owners of cheap shops. They often make a loss on each item they sell, but they tend to sell off their stockpiles more quickly.

Trader on the Day

Scalpers and day traders both concentrate on short-term deals, while day traders have a longer turnaround time. They may make several deals every day (thus the name) since they favor short, 20-minute trades.

Scalpers and day traders both lack substantial funds. As a result, they trade often to lessen the impact of daily losses. In theory, a day trader may survive in challenging circumstances or abandon the market without giving up major investments due to their frequent activity and thin financial base.

Due to their frequent activity, day traders do not maintain positions for very long. Their profit margins are thus quite slim. Their winning criteria are volume-based rather than per-item value, which makes them comparable to scalpers in this regard.

"Swing Trader"

Swing traders are more inclined to hold onto their positions for longer periods of time. Because they lack the time or resources to constantly review their trades, these traders need some faith as well as patience.

Swing traders will hold onto their holdings until the market circumstances improve, as the term suggests. It is referred to as a "market swing." As a result, they need a sizable amount of money to maintain their assets during challenging economic times.

The ability to create higher profit margins when offering their assets for trading is one benefit of not trading often. It is dependent on time, however. A swing trader will be the first to open for business and reap the benefits when conditions start to get better.

Trader of positions

These traders are the definition of "long term." Like swing traders, they are able to put off trading for impossibly lengthy periods of time. Years after buying a stock, a position trader often opens it up for trading. As a result, people prefer to avoid the stock market.

A stock is difficult to withhold because of how the market affects its value. As a consequence, the strategy of a position trader needs a lot of money to live.

But in the end, all of your persistence will be rewarded. Position traders may benefit greatly under the right conditions. A position trader is in the greatest position to make thousands of dollars for each stock moved, albeit this might be ascribed to long-term preparation or the capacity to accurately forecast future stock movements.

The Key Learning:

Simply put, the market's diversity of investor and trading personalities serves as proof that it is inclusive. Everyone has an opportunity to prosper in the market, even though there will always be winners and losers.

The most crucial thing is to choose a look that makes you feel most comfortable or, better yet, confident. To put it simply, if you want to succeed in the stock market, you must play to your strengths. Of course, this assumes that you are aware of your advantages.

The Business Management Must Be Competent.

Successful businesses are the result of vigilant leaders. Business transactions resemble a game of chess. If the management lacks vision, strategic thinking, and appropriate budgeting abilities, the business will fail in the long run as well as the short term. Value investors like Buffett examine a company's debt profile to determine the management's competence. The two crucial ratios to pay attention to are:

Equity to Debt Ratio

The debt-to-equity ratio must be lower than 0.5, or 50%. It may be computed by dividing the total liabilities of the firm by the equity of its owners. Additionally, each organization that does investing research has a website where this value may be readily and gratis retrieved.

Simply defined, a corporation is incurring more debt than is necessary for its financial health if its overall liabilities exceed 0.5 of its entire shareholder equity. If so, you shouldn't invest in that business.

Present ratio

More than 1.5 should be the current ratio. By dividing total current assets by total current liabilities, it may be computed.

A corporation is taking on more debt than it can handle, which is an indication of bad management, if this number is less than 1.5. You shouldn't invest in a firm that has excessive debt.

Rule #2: The product must have a bright future.

Although relatively easy, this step is really important. Recall that purchasing and holding onto a certain stock for a long time is a key component of value investing. According to Warren Buffett, "our favorite holding period is forever."

A firm does not meet the criteria for an excellent stock for value investing if it is now prospering on a product that will be obsolete in a few decades. If it gets outdated, it won't exactly make you a lot of money, will it?

What goods may be thought of as having long-term possibilities at this point? There is no universal solution, because categorizing every product in the world would take a million pages to put in this book. The good thing is that you can decide for yourself since this is usually pretty intuitive.

Just consider it. For instance, food and medicine will both be important. We will always need to eat in order to survive and take medication in order to treat ailments, right? As more nations start to globalize, airlines will also become more important.

In contrast, the field of technology is one that is rapidly developing. To be quite honest, we are unsure of how important this business will be in 30 or 40 years. As a matter of fact, Warren Buffett has said that he does not understand technology investment, which is why he has mostly avoided it. Yes, since their founding, technological companies like FAANG (Facebook, Apple, Amazon, Netflix, and Google) have historically increased quickly. However, just take a look at what occurred in 2018. Globally, tech stocks fell to record lows, wiping off hundreds of billions of dollars in value, including those of Chinese internet behemoths Tencent and Alibaba. We should not invest with great confidence in a market with this level of volatility.

Understanding The Different Types Of Cryptocurrency

When it was initially established in 2009, Bitcoin had practically no competition as a brand-new kind of digital currency. Competitors began constructing their own websites and currencies in 2011 utilizing the blockchain technology that Bitcoin was created on. There was a sudden rush to create additional crypto.

Despite the fact that each cryptocurrency is designed to provide a unique feature or function, the bulk of them are founded on the same ideas as bitcoin:

Cryptocurrency is not created, governed, or supported by a centralized entity like a bank.

These coins are created using peer-to-peer evaluation and blockchain technology.

Bitcoin and other forms of currency are encrypted (secured) using complex computer code known as cryptography.

In digital wallets that allow users manage and trade their coins, such a blockchain wallet, cryptocurrencies are often kept as assets.

As of September 2021, there are an estimated 6,000 to 10,000 different types of cryptocurrencies available for trading, with a total market value of about to $2 trillion.

What kind of cryptocurrencies are available?

Two main categories may be used to categorize cryptocurrencies:

cryptocurrencies, including non-Bitcoin cryptocurrencies and cryptocurrencies like Bitcoin

On the blockchain of a network, there are assets called tokens that may be programmed.

Although the phrases cryptocurrency, tokens, and coins are sometimes used synonymously, it's important to understand the differences between them in order to understand the fundamentals of cryptocurrencies.

• Tokens vs cryptocurrency coins

Despite having different uses, tokens and coins are both sorts of cryptocurrency. Coins are made on their own blockchain and are intended to be used as a kind of currency. For instance, the Ethereum blockchain is the foundation of the cryptocurrency Ether (ETH).

A blockchain-based cryptocurrency called an altcoin is not bitcoin (more on that later).

In contrast to fiat currency, which is based on an already-existing blockchain, tokens are programmable assets that allow for the creation and execution of certain smart contracts. These contracts may be used to create asset ownership outside of the blockchain network. Tokens may stand in for several types of value units, including coins, energy, points, money, and more. They can both send and receive signals.

For instance, the BAT (Basic Attention asset) is an Ethereum-based digital advertising asset.

- Alternative Cryptocurrencies: What Are They?

As an abbreviation for "alternative to Bitcoin," the name "altcoin" was developed, and the great majority of altcoins were developed to enhance Bitcoin in some way. Examples of alternative currency include Namecoin, Peercoin, Litecoin, USD Coin, and Ethereum.

A limited supply of certain cryptocurrencies, such as Bitcoin, helps to increase demand and preserve the currency's perceived value. For instance, the Bitcoin developers set a limit on the number of Bitcoins that may be created at 21 million.

Despite the fact that the majority of alternative currencies share similar characteristics with Bitcoin and are built on the same basic design, each one offers different advantages to investors. Different techniques are used by certain cryptocurrencies to create and validate transaction blocks. Some could provide an advantage, like smart contracts, or further functionality. Others might lessen price volatility.

A process known as an Initial Coin Offering, or ICO, which functions like a stock offering, is often used to create and distribute tokens. They may be stated in the following manner:

Money tokens

Tokens for security

Tokens denote value much as American dollars do, although they aren't nearly as valuable since a token's value isn't necessarily $1. On the other hand, tokens may be used to many other kinds of transactions.

A token differs from a currency in that it is created within the blockchain of an existing coin, like Bitcoin or Ethereum.

2.2 The Top 10 Types of Cryptocurrency

Below is a list of the top 10 cryptocurrencies by market capitalization.

The 2.2.1 Bitcoin

The first cryptocurrency, Bitcoin, was created in 2009 by a person (or maybe a group) going by the name Satoshi Nakamoto.

Bitcoin was designed to operate independently of all national central banks. As an alternative, it makes use of blockchain technology, a decentralized public ledger that records each Bitcoin trade. The peer-to-peer (or agreement) verification technique that forms the basis of modern cryptography was invented by Bitcoin.

Proof-of-work (PoW), a difficult and time-consuming technique, is used by bitcoin miners to verify transaction blocks and create new bitcoins. As a result of the transactions being permanently recorded on the blockchain, each bitcoin as well as the whole network are validated and secured. Environmental concerns have lately been raised since Bitcoin requires a significant amount of energy to produce.

What is the Bitcoin Protocol's Mechanism?

By following the same three rules as traditional, or fiat, currencies, Bitcoin functions as a digital currency.

• They must be challenging to produce (in the case of money) or find (in the case of gold or other precious metals).

• There must be limitations on their accessibility.

- Others must value them and acknowledge their worth.

When we examine Bitcoin, we can observe that it possesses each of these three qualities:

- Bitcoin is produced using intricate computer processes that need a lot of processing power and proof-of-work, making it difficult or impossible to replicate at a cheap cost.

- There are only a certain number of bitcoins—21 million to be precise.

- Numerous Bitcoin exchanges exist, and as of 2015, over 2/3 of this total has been mined. Bitcoin is accepted as payment anywhere from Subway to OKCupid.

Since they get payment in Bitcoin for their computers' labor, bitcoin miners have an incentive to continue mining. Bitcoin was designed to be a deflationary currency, meaning that unlike fiat currencies, the total amount of money is fixed. This assures that no one person or authority can simply issue additional currencies once the supply has been mined, especially when combined with the decentralization idea. The value of the money will, in theory, rise even after all the coins have been extracted.

A digital database called the blockchain is used to track Bitcoin transactions. The fundamental idea supporting the usefulness of Bitcoin is decentralization. Decentralization ensures that no one entity or group controls the blockchain. In actuality, anybody may access it. Transactions are thus publicly broadcast via the network, guaranteeing that each party has upheld their end of the contract. Anyone may see the code since it is publicly accessible (like Windows or

Android), guaranteeing that all parties are informed.

Decentralization enables the blockchain to be protected by several points of entry and hidden by numerous points of failure. As a consequence, incidents like theft and hacking are prevented. For instance, if someone gives you 1 Bitcoin, you may check the blockchain history to be sure it hasn't been spent and is still legitimate. The need for third-party transaction validation is removed by this solution. The only transaction costs are those related to the electricity or computing power needed to maintain the blockchain.

Since Bitcoin has no nation-state, this has a wide range of practical ramifications, from lowering the overall cost of certain commodities to making international transfers more affordable.

As a Wealth Store, Bitcoin

Due to its deflationary characteristics, Bitcoin is a useful investment instrument during hyperinflationary situations. It's likely that Bitcoin, like gold, will be used as a form of money when things become tough financially. Before Bitcoin may be used as money or a store of value, it has to fulfill a few conditions.

• It cannot be perishable; • Its worth cannot deteriorate over time.

The second condition is a bit more debatable since some contend that when more advanced technology replaces Bitcoin, its value may decline. But much like Facebook or email, Bitcoin has come to a stage in the market where the idea itself is valuable. Email isn't particularly useful if you're the only one with an account, but as more people use it, the easier and more valuable it becomes.

Venezuela is going through its worst financial crisis in ten years. Prices have risen to the point that many individuals are unable to buy basic necessities since their money is now almost worthless in compared to the US dollar. Unless you hold Bitcoins, which are becoming more valuable relative to the US currency.

China is doing the same, but for other reasons. Traditional investments in Chinese commodities have produced weaker returns than in previous years as a result of the government's devaluation of the Yuan. Silver and gold exchange rates are tightly regulated, and transaction costs are considerable. Since Bitcoin is resistant to all of these issues, it is often the sole choice for consumers want to safeguard their wealth both immediately and in the long run.

A "safety net" or "hedge" against erratic financial markets has historically been gold. In times of war or financial crisis, gold prices are anticipated to surge while stock markets are in freefall. However, this has not been the situation in recent years. At the time of writing, Gold's 12-month performance has not altered, but Bitcoin has grown by over 1000 percent. Rising tensions in North Korea are just one factor that has hampered Bitcoin's ascent in uncertain times.

There have been more sales from China, Japan, and South Korea as a consequence of the local unrest.

How To Invest In Etfs

ETF (Photo credit: flickr.com)

Exchange-traded Funds (ETFs) combine the money from different investors to buy a variety of assets (such as bonds, equities, commodities, etc.). When the ETF is created, a comprehensive purchase plan for these assets is devised. Similar to stocks, this investment instrument may be purchased or sold during trading hours.

The Advantages ETFs Offer

Diversification - ETFs provide good protection against unexpected price movements since they are made up of a variety of assets. This implies that just by purchasing ETFs, you may instantly diversify your investing portfolio.

Cost effectiveness - Compared to other investment vehicles, ETFs have much cheaper handling and trading expenses. You may put more money into your portfolio since you won't have to pay a lot of transaction costs.

Tax effectiveness - ETFs have comparatively minimal tax obligations. As a result, you will be able to keep more of the money you earn.

Excellent liquidity is offered by this investment instrument. The trading day offers the option of buying or selling it. As a result, you have several chances to profit from your ETFs.

Investment Techniques for ETF Holders

Use it as a tactical investment - If you want to make some short-term changes to your capital allocation, you may use ETFs. ETFs will allow you immediate access to fast and successful trades since they are made up of assets from many marketplaces and sectors. Additionally, they might provide you a versatile and affordable alternative to trade in many market segments without having to pay high transaction costs. However, while making ETF investing selections, you still need to take brokerage costs into account.

Make it the main asset in your portfolio of investments - Exchange-traded funds are used as principal assets by certain investors since they are inexpensive and naturally diversified. You may cover several market segments using ETFs and ensure steady returns. Once these investors have a sufficient number of ETFs, they will add other assets (such as bonds, equities, commodities, etc.) to their portfolio to diversify it.

You may also choose to use ETFs passively. Use it to steady your portfolio. You may just purchase these assets to preserve your investments rather than utilizing them to increase your earnings. You may execute strategic or long-term financial choices with the assistance of the diversity provided by ETFs. ETFs may also rebalance your portfolio if you have portion of your money in risky or aggressive investments.

Use it for hedging reasons - Investors may use a variety of hedging methods thanks to the flexibility of ETFs. To protect oneself against unexpected price drops, for instance, you may purchase inverse ETFs. Inverse ETFs gain value anytime the market price declines. On the other side, if you want to protect yourself against inflation, you may buy "inflation-resistant" ETFs (such those that concentrate on bonds and commodities). Additionally, if you have assets in foreign currencies, you may want to consider using currency ETFs to safeguard your portfolio.

Utilize it to manage your money - ETFs may also be used to "store" your wealth. This kind of asset's purchase and sale are simple. That implies that you may place your money in them while you wait for a better investing plan to emerge. When that occurs, you may easily liquidate your ETFs and utilize the proceeds to make the investments you had in mind.

Use it to harvest tax losses: If your portfolio is diverse, there is a significant possibility that some of your assets will be down and others will be up. The market cycle naturally includes this occurrence. Some investors "harvest" tax losses by taking advantage of these price movements. The taxes you pay on your assets might be seen as investment expenses or losses, according on how it works. As a result, you may deduct them from your realized earnings, which will lower the tax that was charged on your income.

Utilize it to round out your portfolio - As an investor, you could wish to get access to certain assets or market segments without having to obtain the necessary skills. Once they have made significant investments, investors often experience this urge. By purchasing several asset kinds, they want to broaden the scope of their investments. For instance, you could desire to invest in new markets or sectors but you don't know much about them. You may add the assets you want to your investing portfolio using ETFs. By doing so, you may simply add to or finish off your portfolio without having to research the assets included inside each ETF.

Utilize it while moving your portfolio to a different broker - Investors sometimes feel the need to change their financial advisor or asset management. Investors are often forced to let their cash "sit idly" while the portfolio is undergoing change. If that ever occurs to you, you need to invest your money in ETFs as opposed to allowing it to sit idle. Once the changeover phase is through, you may maintain or sell out of ETFs since they are flexible and liquid.

The Value Of Investments

Why It's Important to Invest at Any Age?

The sooner you begin investing, the better off you will be in the long run. Sadly, I started investing after I was almost out of my twenties, but even if you are much older than this, investment is still very important. By generating interest over time passively, investing gives you the chance to increase the overall quantity of your assets. When the benefits of investing are outlined, the case for becoming engaged is pretty strong; the problem is that many of us prefer to utilize money for immediate purposes over saving and investing when the opportunity arises.

One need just consider the penny dilemma, a well-known thought experiment, to show the value of investing vs utilizing your current cash on hand. Which offer—one million dollars immediately or interest accrued on a penny that doubled every day for a month—would you choose? Many people would choose to accept the more immediate payment of one million dollars without giving the issue any thought. Instead of choosing the option with interest accumulating, option one would leave you with approximately 4.5 million dollars less than if you had chosen the second option.

Even while it may not seem like a wonderful method to earn a lot of interest, if you start to analyze the situation and run the figures, you can clearly see that this is the choice that will provide the most returns. The crucial factor is that the penny earns interest exponentially, so even though you may only have two cents on day two, by day eight you will have $1.28. With just $5,242.88 accumulating by day 20, you have not yet reached the first million dollars in earnings, but by day 30, the total pool will have increased to $5,368,709.12 instead. I want you to take away two key points from this instance: One is that interest is not obvious to people, therefore it is difficult to understand how rapidly money may increase unless we carefully arrange the arithmetic and demonstrate the results. Two, waiting 30 days to make much more money was the real expense of not collecting the million dollars upfront. This is a crucial investment idea since all you will be trading to make money rapidly is your time away from your money. Even though you didn't have a million dollars lying around that you could spend for thirty dollars, by the end of the month, you had a lot more money.

The last two components of this case are crucial: what might you have done with a million dollars in those thirty days and what is your tax liability? You'll learn in subsequent chapters that holding a stake in an investment isn't necessarily a good idea if there are alternative chances for your money to grow. There are many real-world situations where you may have earned more on the original up-front cash than leaving money in an interest-bearing account, but it is unlikely that you could have quintupled your money in the penny example within thirty days. If you had kept the $1 million in up-front cash in the account, it might have been invested to earn interest considerably more quickly than the basic amount. You must also take into account your tax obligations with regard to either amount of money. Currently, there is a four and a half million dollar difference between the accounts, meaning that holding a penny in the savings account earns you significantly more money. Imagine if the difference was much less, maybe just $50,000. In this situation, getting a million dollars up front is much more alluring since you stand to earn somewhat more than in the initial scenario. This does not account for the difference in tax obligations between the cash you made immediately and what you would have earned over the course of thirty days. In general, the cost of the tax obligation increases with the speed at which you obtain a return on an investment. The tax obligation decreases the longer you wait. This indicates that if you kept onto the investment for 30 days, you might potentially earn far more than $50,000. This isn't because the initial investment was much greater; rather, it's because the tax rate is much more favourable. This is a microcosmic example, and the real tax obligation is probably the same for small time variations of just thirty days, but there are significant changes for larger time periods.

Additive Interest

You should be aware that although in the ideal world you should take advantage of a bargain that allows you to double your money for a period of thirty days, in the actual world investing is much more challenging. These fantastic possibilities won't come your way so easy. However, the penny example highlights compound interest, a crucial component of investment that enables your money to produce income more quickly. You may earn interest on interest that has already accumulated thanks to compound interest. Despite the definition's complexity, the idea is really rather straightforward. Compound interest is shown in the preceding penny example, although in an impractical context. The money grows at such an exponential pace thanks to the daily doubling of interest accrued on each penny and the fresh total that is multiplying. For a practical illustration, we must choose a far less extreme case.

Imagine if you had one hundred dollars growing at 1% interest, compounded four times a year. The interest you would expect to get at the end of a year would be assumed to be one dollar, or merely one percent of your initial investment, but this is not exactly true. You have earned $0.25, or one-quarter of the one percent interest, after three months since it is compounding and increased to four times annually. It's important to remember that this modest amount is reinvested in the underlying investment so that, during the next interest period, which lasts for another three months, you will be paid interest on $100.25 rather than simply $100. When the first year comes to a conclusion, this has essentially occurred four times. You made $100.25 at the end of the first quarter, $100.50 in the second, $100.76 in the third, and $101.02 in the fourth. Although these figures are not far from the 1% interest you may have first anticipated, you can see that because the interest is compounding, you are really earning more after only a quarter of 1%. You are accruing interest much more quickly since it is being added to the new amount. In this case, the difference is just two cents, but with bigger quantities of money and higher interest rates, the difference may increase significantly.

Additionally, there is a different concept of compound interest, which is the adding of interest from one investment to another. It is up to the person to figure out the specifics since this is less formalized than compounding interest once every quarter. You can see, though, that your interest would increase more quickly if you kept track of all the money you accrued and invested it in other business projects. Compound interest is a concept that allows you to appreciate the value of beginning to invest as soon as you can since it always uses the interest from older investments to carry over to fresh interest. Regardless of the overall amount of your assets, the longer you invest, the better off you will be. It is just impossible to disregard the notion of interest piling on top of interest.

Why You Need to Invest Even If You're Under Financial Stress

Compound interest should be a very convincing case for why you should begin saving as soon as possible, but I am aware of how difficult investing might appear when you are struggling financially. I would have found it impossible to make any kind of investment in my future only a few short years ago. I was earning a little wage in a very expensive city, and since I was spending so much of it on housing, food, and travel, I didn't think investing was worthwhile. This is a widespread mindset that I can understand, but it can also do you harm. As soon as you can, you must begin saving and investing since, over the long term, even little sums of your paycheck invested will result in significant rewards.

Let's use a good American as an example. Imagine a guy or woman working 35 to 40 hours a week at a supermarket. They are over forty years old and earn around $600 each week. This indicates that they earn about $30,000 each year. Even without considering taxes, you are aware that this is a little quantity of money. Because the person you are imagining is middle-aged, it is possible that they have family responsibilities that significantly reduce their income. What if this individual managed to save only $10 each week and utilized that money at the end of the year to start investing? They will only have $520 saved at the end of the first year, but with the advice for small capital investing in chapter two, a modest investment of this size may easily yield three to four percent interest. After two years, this person would have $1060.80, of which $520 is added as new savings in year two and $20.80 comes from accruing interest on the first $520. This person now has $1623.24 after three years, of which around $63 was earned from interest on the first two years of savings. Even though the interest rate hasn't changed, we can see that the interest has rapidly increased from rising at only $20 per year to over $60 per year, an increase of three times. They will have made $2208.17 after year four, $2816.50 after year five, and $3449.16 after year six. This person has now saved more than 10 percent of their annual wage after six years, ten dollars a week, and compound interest.

Imagine what you could save if you saved twenty, thirty, or more dollars each week. Ten dollars is a manageable amount to save each week. In only a few years, that tiny amount may equal a sizable nest egg. Imagine if they had begun saving earlier, say, at age 20 or 30, as opposed to forty. Regardless of your age, and regardless of your ability to save and invest, you must always put away money, no matter how much, so that you can reap the rewards of interest – by merely exchanging time and small savings you can build a sizable nest egg in just a few years.

www.ingramcontent.com/pod-product-compliance
Lightning Source LLC
Chambersburg PA
CBHW050029130526
44590CB00042B/2301